INROADS

To my children

and in memory of my stepbrother
Lance Corporal Nigel David Moffett
killed in action
in Afghanistan, 30th May 2009

CAROLYN JESS-COOKE

INROADS

SEREN

Seren is the book imprint of
Poetry Wales Press Ltd.
57 Nolton Street, Bridgend, Wales, CF31 3AE
www.serenbooks.com

The right of Carolyn Jess-Cooke to be identified as
the author of this work has been asserted in accordance
with the Copyright, Designs and Patents Act, 1988.

© Carolyn Jess-Cooke 2010

ISBN: 978-1-85411-511-9

A CIP record for this title is available from the British Library.

The publisher acknowledges the financial assistance of the Welsh Books Council.

Cover art: 'A Ten-Penny Prophet' by Jamie Baldridge.

Printed in Bembo by Bell & Bain Ltd., Glasgow.

Author's website/blog: www.therisktakersguide.com

Mixed Sources
Product group from well-managed
forests and other controlled sources
www.fsc.org   Cert no. TT-COC-002769
© 1996 Forest Stewardship Council
FSC

Contents

A world with a hundred kinds of home will accommodate a thousand kinds of homesickness.

– Pico Iyer, *The Global Soul*

Accent

Stowaway inflections and locally-produced slang
have passports of their own, a visa for the twang
      that tells me you're not Xhosa
but a Geordie raised in Grahamstown, maybe. It's a blitz
of souvenirs on the ears, the way you bring your bliss
      of home that much closer.

Home? Or everywhere? Like combing coral
or sand and snow globes, or a wave-shaped petal
      from Sydney's Manly Cove
my voice fossils places. The way sound chases
itself in tunnels and halls, the way senses
      fold memory into five

is an accent's suitcase aesthetic. Listen.
There's an address, a postcard in the tone,
      the foreign rhythm
and that emphasis, that accent on the off-beat
which echoes longing clearly; the picked-up place-music speaks
      where you ache to be, with whom.

Open-Mic Night at the Memory Karaoke

Memories restage the past in nostalgia's spotlight.
The mind's golden hits
are fished out of the karaoke box

and dribbled back into the mic,
but with a difference. Contestants stagger
to counterpoint under the influence.

Our first flat gets up. I cringe at the damp-
stains, the broken fire, expect it to sing
controversial recreations

of my dirty laundry. Instead it rings
out bad times without their sting: no loo
for three whole weeks (the crowd finds this funny);

an argument's subtexts in the key of
triviality; slap-stick orchestrations
of an ant-hunt with deodorant.

Next, a Russian doll from Berlin sheds skins
like a girl thinning into silence
until she is lost in mistranslation.

My first car revs speed convictions under
a blare of goth rock. A grand piano
lifts its wing: chords of my mother take flight.

Some recollections are reticent.
The pair of jeans I refuse to throw out
belts out a chorus of friendships but zips

up about its stain. A death and a birth
neck shots of shadow at the bar, refusing
to sink into song, like oil on water.

But most are ecstatic to slide into tune
(whether tone-deaf or drowning-cat)
until I get why Odysseus was tied

to the mast and deafened to the Sirens –
this Juke-Box comfort, sing-along's certainty,
the voice lyrics give to dumb aches,

comprehension so harmonic you could drown
inside its ear. At last, the transparency
of this deafening blast from the past:

...Hit me, baby, one more time...
It wasn't love, babe. Just rhyme...

Second-Hand Words

As Barbara Cartland would put it, I love you madly.
    – Umberto Eco, *The Name of the Rose*

Today is the day of rogue acceptances, when an ear becomes a weir
for the winning word. So watch your syntax. We're
playing frisbee with linguistics on the construction site
of authenticity. It's too late to bolt at the sight
of roses. Summer will come, oozing red,
laden with more hearts for the taking and silences to be read
into. Before I answer, answer this: will it stay this way, a three-tier
terrace of time in a kiss? Will a polished tear
of moon on my finger make you a prince?
For asking, you'll get a full set of finger prints
but not fingers. Try to be more specific.
My hand? Get lost somewhere in the South Pacific
where second-hand words are served with coconut bread.
Love's unoriginal. This is the day where futurity's bred
and the moon's a blow-up dingy I row out to sea
to rinse out my sullied replies. Here. Pick *Oui, Hai, Da,* or *Si.*

Yesterday, I Failed

I failed, and the failing was great thereof.
I failed all the way to the sulphur cliffs of cynicism,
    then bungee-jumped.
I shot a hole in one in failure.
I failed and changed the course of history.
I failed admirably, catastrophically, unremittingly, relentlessly,
    perspicaciously, deliciously, spaciously, and with the dexterity
    of the common impala.
I did not merely stall, pause, or change my mind –
I failed, like any serious attempt at oil painting in a wind machine.
I failed, but the crops did not.
I failed in a field, and filed as I fooled.
I walked right up to failure, kicked it in the shins,
    and insulted its mother.
I fell in love with failure. We got married and raised a family of failures.
I failed to the sum of the square roots of any two sides of an
    isosceles triangle.
I failed in the key of D flat.
I failed my heart out, I failed until my lungs burned, my brain rattled,
    my skin flapped like a rag against my bones and my tongue
    uttered only 'failure'...
I failed, much to the regret of the management.
I went scuba-diving in failure, I camped under failure,
    I hiked to the summit of failure, I painted the floor with superglue
    while failure was sleeping and when it woke up... I laughed.
I failed in several languages.
I added failure on Facebook.
I failed from caveman to Homo Sapiens.
I failed stupendously, outlandishly, biblically, savagely, juicily, Byzantinely,
    heroically, intergalactically.
I failed in hard copy, fax, text, email, Skype, and podcast.
I failed to the soundtrack of James Bond.
I failed as magnesium is to water, as the Apocalypse is to
    a Saturday morning lie-in,
        as Godzilla is to the streets of Tokyo.
I failed, and I failed,
but at least
I tried.

Aeneas Finds Dido on YouTube

I left her at the docks, but before we set sail
I'd a buzzing in my pocket: a video text
of her burning all my clothes, my *Wii*, my *Trojan*
coffee maker. She combed the ashes, then winked.

I descended into the underworld of exes
on Facebook: girlfriends from ten years ago,
school mates I could only recall by nickname,
so many of them bloated and aged

it was like a trawl of filmed corpses.
I clicked on *YouTube*: a hive of live
footage, enough to keep me jived
when the guilt clawed me down

and there she was. White as marble, a train
of ivory silk slipping up the church floor
like a receding tide
and my replacement in black tails

waiting for her at the shore
of the pulpit, a sunrise
of roses, to wed. Although
I was the one who left

I kept returning to her
texts, emails, all the *Post-Its*
she stuck to my *iPod*. So as I watch
her arch into the locking kiss, wifed bliss,

I am docked online, night and day.
And I cannot help but impale myself
again and again
on this arrow marked

'play'

Orpheus Gets Punk'd

They said she was dead. Bitten by a snake:
chainsaw with a brain. They filmed the news
slicing my heart like a special effect.

The plan was to surprise me at the pyre,
have her burst out of flames as though leaping
off a yellow train. Immortality

is real estate, brokered by King Pluto.
So I knew where to go. They don't know
the details of our contract, but I'll tell you.

I mortgaged my future; he bought my past.
He requested my memories, the whole
million reels. Persephone recalled

the seven pips that signed off her pre-nup,
and she relented. I could choose seven
scenes to keep as my own. I chose quickly:

the night we met. The taste of first love dressed
in her kiss. Wedding, owning, missing her.
Re-finding her. And, for a reason I

cannot place – losing her. This most recent
barb was tantalizing as pomegranate,
the tang of quenched fire, the borderline

between breath and death. That was my ticket.
Cerberus heard it in my veins. Dropped, mute.
I entered Hades' darkroom where souls flapped

in eternity like blank pages.
I knew her in all guises: sketch, acrylic.
She was iconic in negative.

She played along to know love's mileage.
All CCTVs on me, I led the way,
recalling the deal. *Do not look back.*

No past. Just continents of remembrance.
But like a Tarkovsky goddess she was
divine in my mind. The close-ups and jump-cuts

symphonic shots of closeness, hours I'd watched her
sleep symbolic images of craving
loss. The stroke of its blade. So I left her,

stuck as a shade. Lived like a *Polaroid.*
Loved in retrograde.

Place

Witness as I drop the kite-angled flint
into the dull lens of pond – almost immediately
circles erupt from the rock's lines,
as though the union of water and stone makes a ghost of straightness
in gaping eye-shaped form. I envy the way the mark is made:
a quick clap but a lasting change in things,
a change in the place of water.

And so it is with us: dropped without applause somewhere
purposefully random, sometimes without identifying
the accuracy of the aim or the blade-like parameter of character,
sharpened to make a mark. And while the eyes might wish
each regrettably wrong curve a cinematic right angle
          the circles we roar will only be seen
as they ring from the roads of our choosing.

Rewriting the Mappa Mundi

When I long for flight and difference
I think of de Bello's mythical atlas,

its accurate designation of the River Oxus,
its fantasy of India's 5000 cities.

And I note the one-footed Sciapod,
the foot-noted Hereford,

and do not find them mythical at all.
Each is reflective

of the ache bowling
an untrespassed world

– with tax-free towns
and edible hills –

that resonates with this vellum's dispute
of greener pastures. And so I rewrite

my own as the one only I have known.

Bitten

The first time I was five. An Alsatian
we teased stripped a layer of skin from wrist
to elbow. It was a blind sensation
the first time. I was five, and all stations
between six and twelve were flagged with lesions
connected, somehow, to a need to be kissed
for the first time. I was five, and satiation,
wet ease, stripped a layer of skin from risk.

The Archer

The archer pulls
    his arm back
drawing the thin string
    to his shoulder

The archer holds my mother
    against the wall by the throat
with his bow-hand
    and drags his fist back

The archer shoots
    so many
        so many
            arrows

Because of That Morning in 1983

I shall bake a cake.

Because I hid under the chipped wooden counter
at the dole office, wondering what 'redundancy' meant,
I shall set out the cream, break a chocolate bar
        into pieces, like a sacrament.

Because my mother paced the hours into the bare
floor, her face tight as dried fruit, I squidge
coins of butter through my fists, think of her
        tap-tapping feet as I sift the flour,

then grate a lemon's belly with a bailiff's mercy
because her pleas shredded into tears
through that multiple-choice, categorically-
        chicken wire grille.

My recipe? An interpretation of how she said
and what she meant by 'seven weeks, seven weeks?'
drawing breath as if hoarding it for the winter,
        and a little ingredient of my own:

all the flavours of that morning and thereafter
melted into one of few kinds of easy richness –
this golden cake, which I shall devour whole,

        just because I can.

Music Lesson

I am seven years old.
The window is filled with my face,
watching for her return. The rain,
globed like semibreves, is a page of music.

I know nothing but deafness
at the end of those fists,
a fists's *sforzando*
pummelling the white keys black.

The window is a stave
ringing all the captive notes' ransom.
They cling to their bars,
too afraid to leave.

The conductor is so black and white,
he sees only right and wrong.
I am his wrong.
You are the conductor,

waving your arms to the rhythm
of your rage.
I stand here, mute as a page,
waiting for the cadence

of a chair in the air
or another broken door
and the tiny, awe-filled applause
of rain against the window

before she comes home
to the Grand Finale.
How well you know this music!
You heard it often as a child

falling beautifully on the walls'
decidedly deaf ears.
You grew to love the black and white,
you knew then where you stood

with him, your own father.
Every silence must be filled
with a cadenza,
and I, your echoing coda,

must be filled with the din
of your scars
that cry out their unheard melodies
at the ends of your muffled wrists.

The window wells up with tears.
There is a change of key.
You behind me
beating time with a belt.

One Thousand Painful Pieces

At every water-edge I think of new shipments
and exiles whose too-mobile reflections
drowned a face and founded a city
whose same abandonment – the portrait of leaving –
floods from the black
plastic hollow of the suicide they're zipping up before me –

the portrait of leaving. The face my father wore
the first time he tried
                            plunging down the stairs, one thousand painful pieces
rippling at his wrists

Daisy

White   petals   lodged   beneath   the skin
         or   cling film   gathered   where air
                              is   trapped   no
hundreds of   scarred   slashes   from her wrist to elbow
          I stagger
          a stare   across   many   glances   like   sketches
on   page corners   that become   a film   when flicked
               I piece   together   an image
 most have been   quick   fire   staccato   pecks
          of   blade
                    others   are   blood   pictures
a   wave   a star   a   coffin   a crocodile
writhes   on   her extensor   symbol   of   the   way   pain
          can   drag   roll and   hold   prey   under
I cannot   imagine   turning   the blade   on myself
          I   cannot   imagine   becoming   the   beast
          but what I   do   know   is
          abuse
is   not   a flame devouring   not a   meteor   landing   but
                    a daisy
          in   a storm   its   shattered   petals   wheeling
          the   full   length   of   lineage
          arriving   as   hundreds
of   knives   in the   soul

Pure

Stained glass, broken window watches memories burn
an ocean. Love, you're knee deep, enough to drown:
they chase like hounds, hard lessons to learn.
Stained glass broken, window watches, memories burn
and crush to powder, compound me, a statue waiting to turn
human. You'll not love until I'm pure, contracted as a frown.
Stained. Glass broken. Window watches memory's burn-
ing ocean. Love: your need, deep enough to drown.

Lip Service

The flame is ripping itself up
    but the brand won't quit, remaining even when I close my eyes.
There are degrees of damage in its nearness
    that may be compared to a kiss that becomes a drowning:
the pinking of cheeks, puckered blisters with a wetness
    in touching, a desire to hasten past the layered, delaying skins of
                         experience
right to the bald bones of essence, and then to reverse whatever
                         loves it
    to a shredded pastiche of its origins. It has the movement
of a language in process, or are those letters
    rhythmically whispering shadows into space,
the most precarious of contracts?

Then there's that mouth, the sort that is utterly makeup-less
    but always bitten-red, cackling under wood as though its taste
were an impish ghost,
    the sort of lips that travel less to a grin than to the half-smile of a
                         pleased spine,
the kind that won't divorce from a kiss before it starts to ulcer,
    and never ever love a thing until it melts, melts into water.

Belmopan, Belize

It is raining. I tell him to slow down.
On either side of the bridge

seventy feet of stiff rock
and a swollen river at the bottom.

When he brakes
the sound of wounded dogs

the car thrashing like a shark
in the stark confines of a net.

I think of crash-test dummies.
A hard slam and a paralytic stasis.

My airbag sleeps snug in its tight jar.
He is silent beside me.

Suddenly I'm padding on glass outside
I don't notice I'm barefoot.

The car is an accordian.
It hisses deep discordant cadences.

He is still in the car and starts to scream.
There is an unseen yoke

on my shoulders. I can't stand straight.
My stomach burns and bleeds.

The soldiers arrive abruptly
barking Creole at the yelling American

and the dazed Irish girl
hunched on the bridge-edge.

They don't know I'm fighting the urge
to faint and trying to see the funny side.

In the wheelchair a nurse rams me
straight into a doorframe on the way to X-ray.

All night I watch a fly frantically headbutt
the invisible boundary of a hospital window.

At the airport my mother reaches anxiously at my neck
where, giraffe-like,

a cast bridges my head to my shoulders:
a bruised, almost-broken distance.

Tourists

departing from 'The Whitsun Weddings' by Philip Larkin

That Sunday, we were late getting away.
    Round about
one-twenty pm on the fogged runway
our three-quarters-full Qantas flight took off,
all blinds down, all meals hot, everyone tense
as we'd been delayed nine hours. We pulled up
over the knuckled flat blocks, watched as streets
webbed and rippled to the docks, saw the dense
outline of Bangkok turn into a step
on the river where rain came down in sheets.

Most of the afternoon, you read, I slept
    for about a thousand miles
as the plane curved southwards. Your wide arms kept
wrestling with pillows; you let canals
of light pour in on top of me to see
the frothy clouds squashing Sumatra. I
was bored of my book; its vernacular
was to me an escape velocity
of driftwood ideals. As planned, the moth-sky
fluttered its wings, poured a funicular

of silver water on the plane window.
    Some tourists made
a big fuss about the flashing solo
streak that had crackled behind a cloud's shade,
how it danced along the long cool platforms
of the edge of the sea. I was sleeping
but the turbulence woke me; not until
I watched immigrants larking with green forms,
Hollywood marrieds dripping in bling
and passionate honeymooners, all

turned out for their touristic event
    without waving goodbye
to where they were from, resolutely bent
on sporting their courtship identity,
did I consider us in different terms:

I used to love seeing lovers that looked
alike, as though they'd adopted the same
expression, halves of one reflection, forms
of one person, showing to the whole world
their union, that they played for the same team.

And it seemed to me that this mimicry
        proved the ways
we view love as home, how we marry
that ideal, backpack it, soak up its rays
without sunblock. You and I didn't resemble
each other at all, but we both agreed
that *real* love looks in the same direction.
Yet the common ground we'd tried to assemble
was on a fault line, and when the earth frowned
islands would form like the hottest fashion.

I always liked travelling further
        than the less deceived:
an agoraphobic explorer,
I'd cling tighter when I needed to leave.
And so, when the plane rocked to and fro,
when the spiky phalanges of heaven
drummed on the plane wings, I reached for your
arms to feel the safety of limbo,
the way we always held firmly when
love landed us in unfamiliar

territory. We weren't your average
        tourists, dying
for long exposure shots of the Taj
Mahal or any artifice that sung
of eternity; we had jointly,
silently, agreed to take day trips
to love, picnicking there, testing out
its restaurants oh so trepidly.
We'd wade out in it, up to the hips,
but never really wanted to get wet.

Sydney airport loomed: there we were aimed.
    Bright knots of rail-
grey clouds sulked behind us. Post-storm, you seemed
no more than a pair of arms. The rain-veil
lifted, I could see the ground and wanted
not to know it, I was ready to be loosed
with all the altitude that love can gain.
I felt my brakes tighten; we had landed
but, for once, no sense of falling. Like a guest,
the storm departed, somewhere becoming rain.

Jet Lag

Whatever circadian rhythms were meant to coax
my body back to regularity flew
their rickety cage last week. I'm a rained-on leaf,
bug-eyed at seven, seven mornings after landing,
living on *Rennies* and aspirin. The pattern
is this: my rage to sleep

is my built-in prevention of sleep.
I've named the sheep, stopped drinking Coke,
yet find myself studying the carpet pattern
with the seriousness and drowsiness of the 'flu.
I'm a nightly visitor to our landing,
up and down the stairs until consciousness takes its leave.

My eyelids flap open and shut like leaves
in north winds. Nothing else will do but to sleep
off the gnawing belly-ache that struck upon landing,
the piercing nausea, an alien mole I tried to coax
out of my mouth with a gentle tonsil-prod that flew
to the stomach-pit, forming a hard roundness. This pattern

of prodding and bloatedness is nothing compared to the pattern
of blue circles that halo the room when I leave
my chair, a rocky sensation akin to flying,
the pendulum feeling that's meant to come before sleep.
I treat myself so gently now, as though I'm coaxing
a fragile other, a five-year old after landing

on her chin from her bike, a bruised and bloody touch-down.
The dark circles and twitching eye have become such a pattern
I start to think I'll miss it, miss the wired vacantness of
                              too many Cokes
and the blood-red thread-veins of a leaf
that fill my eyes instead of sleep.
It's enough to make me wonder why I ever flew,

why I didn't try a ferry or train instead of flying.
The elusive chute into unconsciousness, landing
among the grimmest of nightmares, even bad sleep
is a touch-down devoutly to be wished. This pattern
of cramping, shotglassed *Gaviscon*, having to leave
the room suddenly is nothing I'll have to be coaxed out of.
Yet jet lag has no predictable pattern.
No previous landing has made me light-sensitive as a leaf.
I dream of next month's flight as codeine-free,
of sleep, of moles, of *Coke*.

Reading Mt. Fuji's Diaries

In 50-denier fog sight is stockinged
    and shapes become text to be read
by proximity: *katakana* fir trees,
    the summit-bends' slicing orthography,
my own palm splayed before my nose
    with all the meanings your first valentine
groped towards. Within the drapes
    of Fuji's curtained off-stage
I find whispered testimonies
    and maps of silence. Some voices are sheathed.
The juddering coach no more than a purr.
    The mountain is lost in lunar confessions,
streams of spectral palimpsests without seams
    touristed in hope that the spine
will offer up a window to her capital
    'A'. Closure brings the whole alphabet.
Outside the pyramid are murals
    vivid as revived pharaohs, disclosures of desire.
Columns of this silky sun-sheened screen
    project wet-ink memories of how our scene
came slowly into focus. In writing
    there's a clearing, the pout-puffed parchment
and *kanji*-ed *mise-en-scène*
    speaking to me now the way passion is penned
at the beginning in single digits:
    the first nicks of rain on ocean skin
sketching mists of recognition,
    love's bones under X-ray.

Waterfall at Lake Chuzenji, Japan

Light skims the guillotine blade of the waterfall
as it slices through fog, all to the roar of a god's boiling kettle.
Rock spools blank celluloid from the lake's pool
    of reflections. It's the one thing to fall

and never land. They say the unmarried come here
to drown themselves. The monkeys are
indifferent. They are used to wet mist like milk gone sour,
    the unlit lamp-leaves, the water's hour

hand unmoving from noon as if time had stopped.
This is the face of love that's sinister, the desperate leap
because falling won't happen to all of us. The cup
    can be filled, the spoon can be heaped

to its limits and neither will drop. It's the spill
over into sureness, something equal
and measured into two halves that is the water level
    of permanence, the difference between all

or nothing, the dimension of always. Leaves keep
mimicking the sound, wishing to simmer. There's no set way to slip
into this, but walking takes two legs. Don't quit. Look at the lone rip
    of falling lake: it keeps trying to stand up.

First Time Buyer

So *this* is what I get for wanting to stay
somewhere more than a few months, for wanting
to buy a mat that says HOME instead of a ticket
to SYD or IST or NYC or any three-letter combo,
switching – maybe – to MRS, one grounded half
of a stamped and hyphened surname.
I'm only buying because I know
I can sell, you know, because this ladder
is apparently a one way street
for those in the know, and because I woke up one morning
and realised that the word *home* had no image behind it,
that I'd attributed one word in one language and one dialect
to countless continents, countries, streets, people.
Surely this would result eventually in a crisis of identity?
Surely a mortgage is the only means
of purchasing my own two feet,
a doorbelled 'I am (here) (after six)'
at which my other 'homes' can stay?
As a first time buyer, I must navigate
the well-chartered territories of mortgage percentages
instead of map coordinates, I must commit
to a black roof and grey walls
with no sun-scorched view for which I'll pay
the same as a roundtrip to NYC every month until I'm sixty-three,
to live on the ground floor instead of mid-air,
to pay parking fines instead of excess baggage,
to date instead of counting dates,
to hold someone's hand instead of luggage,
to carry with me – maybe – a *life*,
to house another,
to be someone's wings, roof, gate, one way street
and three-letter combo,
should they choose to stay. Should they choose to stay.

Boo!

Do you name your shame in a moment of surprise?
Why put on, even for a *Kodak* second, the guise

of worm-brained despair before cheery bravado
at scaring me out of my wits, shaking my cherry-red composure

by hiding behind the door? You make me think of unawareness
as a trampoline swiped mid-leap, a pool drained during a dive,

tectonic rifts under the Tyne, our baby's first postcard as an extra line.
Despite 50 meg broadband, instant mash and predictive text

I expected miracles to inch like blue whales up the M4
humping all the way to my tomb-stoned door.

5 Months

I expand like a book in water.

The skin a road map, the chest grooved
by tattoo-blue streams of liquid
as if escaping a smashed inkwell.

The slow soufflé of the abdomen
rises as a kite
jerks upon unseen currents.

Note the bronzing clappers of belled breasts
seasoning with sound:
from these the unstemmed fruit will trumpet out
white rivers of pure expression, word–embryos.

And not all of it physical!

A small blue crown
on the gas hob
unnoticed all day.
Shoes stacked
in the fridge.
    Focus   flapping
in the mind's lampshade

dazzled day and night by the bulb
that books said *now a brazil nut,*
now a lemon. Then

there was the bear I dared to stir
with smells, who stood up on two legs
and roared in a basin for seven weeks.

While the bear rested
a new skin
rippled in a tempest, weathering creation.

Each day now this skin is shed and re-grown, ripening
my body's sealing clasp
that holds and lets go, holds and lets go
around a second heartbeat.

Once, I saw my mother rip, cut, tear and sew
a curtain to make me Cinderella.

That may be what is asked.

For now, I am linen
tossed in a tidal gale
and all the shapes
                it makes
                    in falling

Newborn

What are you like?

A minute old, you're a sky-blue candle
quarried from the fire, beeswax on my belly,
then a nub of warm dough

and in the basket by my bed you're
a bag of ripe peaches, soap-bubble fragile,
a slow-waving field fattening with wheat

and at the breast you're a zoo of verbs
mewling, snuffling, pecking,
wolfing, then coiling

into sleep, where you're a water-wheel
churning ancestral reflections
in the journeys of your face

until it's morning and you're unleashed
light, a pinking pearl, a key turning
in the lock of clocked breath

filling our house with hows –

how did the soul arrive there? like a stitched wish
or the way the wind winds itself
into the sea's receiving skin

or did life find you, invite you
to climb to the nib
of the wick and, if so,

what flame set you alight?

Descartes' Daughters

I loved you from the second time you were born.

It was difficult at first. I could not see
the soul sealed in soil.
Then my face rose in yours.
Bout de chou. Déjà vu.

How you worked us with the whip of your wail!

Each night I would uncurl the wave
of your little fist, terrified of still waters.
You said *papa.*
Red mouths opened

on your neck, the pale staircase of your spine,
right down to your knees.
They all kissed you.
And the sea laid flat its hands.

I could not accept the second body they dug for you.

They placed you in like a root.
Leaves
        poured from me.

Your soul was tossed into the air like a small bird.
I made a cage to re-capture it.
Not a doll, not a statue. A reflection
in reverse.

It was difficult at first. We did not remember each other.

But then your marble eyes fluttered,
the mechanistic jerks
of your right-angled limbs
became fluent in the language of memory.

Our first moments returned like migrating birds:

the skin-tent you made with your foot inside,
a red-tinged river, the cervix folding back
like a bridge at the sight of ships. So real,
as if it had been me who gave birth to you.

We set sail at the Queen's request.

There were rumours onboard of ghosts and devils.
The men brought dogs and gunpowder,
opened your box.
Disbelief throttled the sails.

You held out a small white hand. A wave
reached back.
I lost you, lost you.

Now a father surfaces each night in my soul.

Inside every breath
the gradual opening
of wings.

Dorothy's Homecoming

I. Auntie Em

She came to us at six months old: still too young
to call anyone 'mother' and amazed
by her own feet. I recall how they glowed

through her hands as she rocked on her back,
plucking them, until one day she stood up
and walked off to pluck red roses instead.

I tried all variations of the same name:
mother, mama, mummy, mom. She chose 'Em'
like a verbal hesitation, naming

her uncertainty. Who was I to her?
Until she left, I think I was the ghost
of her mother. Once, she said she saw one

of a person who was still alive.
I understood then that I was the double
exposure of her abandonment.

When she came back she saw her own face
in the window before she saw mine, wrote
on the glass what I thought was my name

but was 'home' spelled backwards. Now she knows
the rose has many names. Her feet tour its colour.

II. The Wicked Witch

Child, I told her, there's no going back.
The playfields of your youth will be shopping malls,
a theme park barnacled on the open plains.

I was talking from experience.
My attempts to re-migrate turned me
into shadow, a pseudo-rainbow

scowling into the past. Home as I knew it
had packed its bags, leaving me to broom it
as citizen of the skies. And she did the same.

Hauled away in his balloon, crowned an empress
of transition. Does she know it? No more,
I think, than she understands the writings

of her feet on this new land's text, scribbling
her belonging. I was doing her a favour
by locking her up, stopping the pendulum

pattern of her to-ing and fro-ing. But
she vaporized me on the spot. And I
thank her. There's no exile in the air.

Now she's made it, I can't help but ask her:
how does it feel to be homesick at home?

III. The Twister

I had only ever been a bodice
for so many corpses: the skeleton
of a house, shelled-out cars, the half-bodies

of branchless trees and arms of lightning.
Sounds had silenced in me, sometimes sunlight
bled through, but never before had anything

stepped willingly into me to be gloved
and led, like a fish in the grip of water,
where I saw fit to dissolve. I was love

to her, and not just any kind. The *source*.
I did what I always do, but as tender
as possible. I balmed her with remorse

instead of storm, cradled her with rivers
of light which, before, would have mummified.
I had always believed myself averse

to nurturing until terrified by her loss.
She dropped from my nest, broke the skin around
her dreams. I shattered into rain. Now our roles

are reversed. Some days, she inhales me
in her questions. In her answers, I breathe.

A Poem Without Any Vegetables

She has recently been made a sister. At the far end of the bread aisle at Sainsbury's she roots herself to the spot when I call her name, her soft bruised legs planted wide, arms flat to sides, chin to chest. Her brother is a snoring spud in his car seat, sprouted on top of the trolley. I nudge a few agitated jam-browsers as I make for the milk. I call again. Once or twice she looks up to check I'm still there before quickly re-fixing her gaze on her toes. I stomp towards her. She splats on the floor. People are staring. I crouch down and hiss, 'Come with mummy.' She spits the pips of her vocabulary in retort: 'No. Can't.' I pick her up, bundle her into the trolley amongst the groceries, then push us blindly to the checkout, by which time she's left a trail of flung leeks, lobbed broccoli, speared carrots, chucked Pak Choi and a soil-spewed basil plant from aisle one to twenty-four, and is calm, having won.

Asda, Ten Days Post-Partum

At the fish counter I crawl in among the plaice,
    wrap myself in herring, doze off on pillows of ice.
What do I dream about? Hazard a guess. Days
    sopped in milk and blood, gauzed
in a pre-snooze, puppet-slung from the cobweb-thread
    of consciousness, inanimate as bread.
Whether face-down in ciabatta dough
    or elbow-propped on a tub of *Haribo*
I am still awake, no, sniffer-dog primed, our boy buoying
    me up with his kettle squeals, his mossy head bobbing
on bantam-egg shoulders, his semi-smile
    a red slice of morning at the roller-blind's hem, all
between long trips to the Isle of Nod
    where sense dictates I should join him. Instead

    I'm pronged on the been-there-done-that
of the second child, hooked on an auto-pilot
    expertise in nappy changing, single-handed,
in the dark, while breast feeding; anxieties disbanded
    by our firstborn's foreshadowing
of reflux, hoax-SIDS. Burping.
    Why would I sleep when I'm waist-deep in forensics,
dissecting the maternal bond, excavating the subtexts
    of Gina Ford? Second time round, the fog is gone:
boat trips through baby blues suddenly have a shore line,
    a changing room mirror throws back my body's plowed loam
as a harvest that will be re-sown. Knowing that the plum-
    bottom cupped in my palm will shortly squirm out of sight,
that the tulip mouth will soon turn to other light,

    I dream of snoring among the onions, what that feels like.

Pamukkale, Turkey

From a distance it is cotton
    fat with air, or a castle of cloud
        with a peacock drawbridge of travertine
    terraces lipping down the white slide.
So much ripeness from erosion

has got me wondering what else
    could flower in its own afterlife,
        how corpulence could awake in the corpse-
    pale limestone oozing over the cliff?
Wax should snooze without flame, but melts

here in its absence all the same.
    Walking unsteadily in bare feet
        through chalky rivers I toe honeycomb
    patches of wear and tear, tourist grit.
Some parts have clearly suffered from

visitation, while others strive
    in their unwinding of organ pipes
        and swan-necked formations as if to prove
    that struggle can be graceful, that hope
is the hue of being alive.

I stroke the moon throats, photograph
    the waterfalls transforming to bone.
        The sun's chrysalis unfolds its tough love.
    I leave, re-made, head for the ruin-strewn
pools at Hierapolis to bathe

in life-preserving minerals.
    Here, hacked stems of ancient columns turn
        green underwater. Stars scatter their pearls.
    At dawn, when snowy veins burn crimson,
the mountain exhales its petals.

Fifteen and a Quarter Things to Do With Your Past

1. Dump it in a field when no one's looking and leg it.

2. Pretend, with aid of convenient addiction, that it didn't happen.

3. Mount it on canvas and display on chimney breast.

4. ~~Pin it to blazer/cardigan/left nostril.~~

5. Regret it every Saturday night after a dodgy curry.

6. ~~Recount it word-for-word to every poor sod in earshot.~~

7. Purée and feed it to the rising generation.

8. ~~Filter through Hindsight; purge embarrassing bits.~~

9. Add water. Apply to brick. Build wall. Eventually construct fortress.

10. Stage as musical. Re-perform parts that still don't make sense.

11. ~~Marry it.~~

12. Study it at University.

13. Mail it to unoccupied turkey farm in east Azerbaijan.

14. Climb it, with Sherpa if possible. Stick flag into summit.

15. Recycle. Cut off top, fill with soil, plant seeds. Water.

¼. Let it grow into

In Defence of Multiple Handbags

Furthermore, there is the aesthetic pleasure
of a squad of sacks, swooped by hip or rib,
a minx-pink speech bubble for the subtext
of our sex: wife, sister, five years younger,
always pockets deep enough to bury my mother.
And O! for pragmatics: how else would I cart
solutions for every quandary? How would
I tackle the Olympics of family, work, and miscellany
without lipstick-javelin, *iPhone* shot-put, *Mastercard* rally?
There is sense in not leaving the house without
a cohort of womb-ish carriers, room enough for a canoe,
some small as your hand, others big as changing rooms
in colours that contextualize Suffragette stripes,
sequins to constellate the myths of girlhood, one or two
mannequin-thin totes, the way my body's meant to be
and this tattered hold-all, stuffed to the rafters with laddered
tights, unposted letters, keys to frozen locks: femininity.

Clouds

Catching sight of birds, the white fingers
of Ocean began to dream of better things.
Tired of travelling to and from one side of the world
to the other, they imagined places
beyond their allotted four corners.

The discontented pulled down
Earth's forebodingly fortressed borders;
a coalition of rivers
gnawed at the bank's tight walls.
The once smooth cliff's clawed
ceiling chinked the laddered
thirst of the clouds' indefatigable resolve.

Sagging, soaked, the pale pioneers
dragged their bulk to the highest peak.
Some soon quit; others dropped and chose
instead to crawl over lawns at dawn and evenings.
So few, so few clung to their aim.

At the cliff's summit a small gathering
looked tentatively up, then down.
What a way to fall! Without trying,
there is no knowing, one suggested.
Shunning hesitation, the bravest of the
crowd stepped forward, jumped off,
and flew.

Three Ways to Look Through a Telescope

I. The Usual Suspects

The space-metropolis is under scrutiny. Four-
eyed schoolkids aim Santa's refractor and spy
the usual suspects hopping, swagged and crow-barred,
into black holes. Hard-boiled, they know a Pulsar
when they see one. The game's over for Astronomy.

No one'll rat on Don Big Bang. His dogma lingers on your TV.

II. L-Plates

Galaxies crash at 300,000 mph and lazily leave
the scene; Aurora Borealis dutifully drapes red
tape and sends the shaken supernova back to school.
Solar winds drag the L-plated spiral's busy
street-lamped freeways to the scrap heap for recycling.
The cracked conch-headlights spew astral gas.

The problem with space is there's no marked lanes.

III. In Cognito

Many galactic havens adopt an elaborate disguise.
Zorro-masked, Vegas-feathered, bedecked

with turquoise sequins, they'll pass off
a coiled, tri-sunlit paradise as bushes

of torched gorse on the unsuspecting lens.
Who wants tourists like us? Before Hubble

the others tiptoed past, sneaking their velvet
diamond cases past the airport X-ray with a whistle,

wink and nudge. With UV, their number's up.
Still, the clever ones swear the mirror's smeared

with licked sugar on candy floss.
It takes specific kinds of light to detect them.

One by one, the hoards – a hundred billion or so –
line up under reds, blues and greens. Now known,

the telescope coins a reachable horizon.

"Daily I Forget To Live"

Daily I forget to live.
The defining moments of my life
no more define the quotidian and tedium

than water defines itself. You know
water is shaped by its limitations,
a sculpture perpetually re-set and re-edged

by physical context. The wind too
is a carousel for voices. Where
is its own? Within all those

it carries. Like my life,
so often displaced
by the processes of living, its costs

and injustices and agonies. Sometimes
my life wanders into the moment
when our daughter staggers across

the living room wearing just a nappy
and her father's shoes, spitting vowels
into my mobile phone,

or – never more in focus – when
she is a hot coal, panting with fever at 3am,
so pale and limp between us

it's a kind of anaesthetic to everything else.
But so often I forget all this,
forget my promises to be more patient,

to diet, recycle, meditate, vote.
Sometimes I feel myself get up
from the shed skin of forgetting

heavy and floored like a scaled bark
and for that moment I am weightless as water
alive in the loves that flood me.

Inroads

My vein stands up to the mike and sings out a long red note.
I'm at the clinic giving blood, giving what I half-forgot
was brushed under my carpet
of skin at birth, the life-force quietly
moving through cracks under my surface
and now under the spotlight of a nurse's badge
in a sunset, on-stage, belting out a full vial
of velvety Joni blues.
It is shocking that it pours so willingly, that so much births
from the pore hole, but then it seems
that the blood is a kind of blade
parting the air around it
rivering through so much whiteness
and is almost umbilical: the perfect, original expressway
that flew from my mother and her mother to me,
the rich blue-red road
that echoes now on the inside of my elbow,
knocking at my skin.
I wish I could become this knife, or at least find a way to mimic
the tuning fork of the needle
that summons the silence of my body to sing.
I wish I could follow the end of the road of blood
that leads not to death
but to all things, to the unseen atom-cloth
from which they cut me and sewed me inside to be cut out again,
to the moment of the wish of me,
over the hip-swept dunes to the nebulae nurseries where bone
and tissue and blood weave the soul's coat.

    *

You were born of a dying star
so all the melodies of time could storm through your veins,
so the silence of inertia would be drowned
in the aria of your dreams.
Now sing.

Notes

p. 14. Virgil's Latin epic poem *The Aeneid*, composed during the 1st century BC., tells the story of Trojan warrior Aeneas who, amongst other adventures, fell in love with Dido, the Queen of Carthage. Prompted by the gods to set sail for Sicily, Aeneas abandoned Dido, who swiftly threw herself upon Aeneas' sword. Knowing nothing of Dido's death, Aeneas later visits the underworld. Here he finds Dido, and appeals for her forgiveness. Virgil's text tells it thus:

Talibus Aeneas ardentem et torua tuentem
lenibat dictis animum lacrimasque ciebat.
Illa solo fixos oculos auersa tenebat
nec magis incepto uultum sermone mouetur
quam si dura silex aut stet Marpesia cautes.
Tandem corripuit sese atque inimica refugit
in nemus umbriferum, coniunx ubi pristinus illi
respondet curis aequatque Sychaeus amorem.

With such words Aeneas tried to soothe her passionate, wild-eyed spirit and stir her to tears. But she, turning away, kept her eyes fixed on the ground, nor did she change her expression as he began to speak any more than if she were a hard flint or an immovable crag of Marpessus. At last she started and fled back, still estranged, into a shade-bearing grove where Sychaeus, her husband of long ago, comforted her suffering and returned her love.

p. 15 The word 'punk'd' here refers to the popular hidden-camera TV series, *Punk'd*, which first aired on MTV in 2003, and which featured practical jokes played on celebrities 'who deserve it'. The narrative re-imagines the Greek myth of Orpheus, who, having lost his wife Eurydice to a snake bite, visited the underworld to appeal for Eurydice's return. When he successfully convinced his hosts that they should let her go, he was instructed not to gaze upon her until he made his way back to the mortal realm. Too anxious for her safe return, he turned and gazed upon her – and she vanished.

p. 18 Completed around 1300 AD, Britain's Mappa Mundi is less a geographical map of the world than an exercise in the cartography of idealism, hope, and spiritual salvation.

p. 24 The title of this poem is taken from a comment by Lithuanian filmmaker and poet Jonas Mekas, on leaving a European displaced persons' camp for America: "I wasn't surprised when, upon my arrival in New York, I found others who felt as I felt [...] – people who were also walking like one thousand painful pieces."

p. 42 French philosopher René Descartes' daughter Francine was born in 1635. Descartes was hesitant at first to acknowledge her as his daughter, born out of wedlock to a household maid named Helene Jans. However, when Francine died from scarlet fever at the age of five, Descartes claimed it as the greatest sorrow of his life. Soon after, Descartes is said to have built an automaton, or mechanical doll, in the exact image of his dead child. He also named the doll 'Francine'. The creation of the automaton appears to fuse Descartes' conflicted parental grief and his notions of the soul, expressed in his *Traité de l'homme* (Treatise on Man): "I suppose the body to be nothing but a statue or machine made of earth, which God forms with the explicit intention of making it as much as possible like us."

'*Bout de chou*' translates literally as 'a bit of a cauliflower', but has its equivalent expressions in English with 'honey' and 'sweetheart'.

p. 48 Gina Ford is a controversial 'child guru', whose many books on the subject of child-raising range from *The Contented Little Baby Book* (1999) to *Good Mother, Bad Mother* (2006).
SIDS = 'Sudden Infant Death Syndrome', or cot death.

p. 49 Pammukale, or 'cotton castle', is the result of underground volcanic activity which created hot springs, the mineral content of which has created thick limestone stalactites, potholes and cataracts. Situated near Izmir, Pammukale and its neighbouring (ancient) city Hierpolis form Turkey's two UNESCO World Heritage Sites.

p. 53 In a recent article published in *National Geographic*, astronomer John Dubinski stated that "the Milky Way and Andromeda galaxies are hurtling toward each other at 300,000 miles (480,000 kilometers) an hour. [...] Prognosis for our solar system: either flung safely into space – or blasted by radiation from supernovae at the center of the new galaxy."

Acknowledgements

Thanks are due to the Tyrone Guthrie Centre for a prize in 2005 which facilitated a residency at the Varuna Writers' Centre in Katoomba, NSW, Australia, to the Society of Authors for an Eric Gregory Award in 2005, to the Arts Council of England for a Writers' Award in 2006, and to New Writing North for a Northern Promise Award in 2008. This collection was carouselled into existence by the financial support and, most importantly, the little lights of hope provided by these organizations.

Thanks also to the editors of the following publications in which some of these poems appeared in various guises: *Ambit, Magma, Poetry London, THE SHOp, Poetry Ireland, Black Mountain Review, Stand, Tower Poetry, The Stinging Fly, Women's Work: Modern Women Poets Writing in English* (Seren, 2008), *The Lonely Poets' Guide to Belfast* (Belfast: New Belfast Arts Initiative, 2002), *The New Creative* (Sunderland), and *Poetry Wales.* 'Music Lesson' won second prize in the 2001/2002 Academi Cardiff International Poetry Competition. 'Pure' was engraved into a glass sculpture commissioned by New Belfast Arts' Initiative in 2003.

Thanks, finally, to those whose encouragement and guidance have shaped this work, from its embryonic stages to the final editorial nitty-gritty: as a student at the Queen's University of Belfast, Sinéad Morrissey, Medbh McGuckian and Carol Rumens. In Australia, Deb Westbury, Peter Bishop, Carmel Williams, and my fellow Varunans. In England, Colette Bryce for careful editorial advice, and Olivia Mantle for the French translation. Thanks also to Jamie Baldridge for letting me use his stunning photo as my cover image. Special debts of gratitude are owed to my late grandmother, Anne Stewart, to my mother, Carol Stewart Moffett, to my husband, Jared Jess-Cooke, and to our children, Melody and Phoenix, for their love and inspiration.

About the Author

Carolyn Jess-Cooke was born in Belfast in 1978, and currently lives in Newcastle, where she teaches Creative Writing at Northumbria University. She received an Eric Gregory Award and the Tyrone Guthrie Prize for Poetry in 2005, a major Arts Council of England Award in 2006, and a Northern Promise Award for Poetry in 2008. Her poems have appeared widely in magazines, hand-bags, T-shirts, a glass sculpture, on a perimeter wall for a housing development in Durham, and on a 700m steel floorscape in Middlesbrough. Her first novel, *The Guardian Angel's Journal*, is forthcoming from Little, Brown in 2011. The author's website/blog: www.therisktakersguide.com.